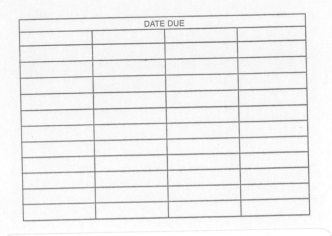

Action Art

Drawing

Isabel Thomas

Heinemann Library
Chicago, Illinois

© 2005 Heinemann Library
a division of Reed Elsevier Inc.
Chicago, Illinois

Customer Service 888-454-2279

Visit our website at www.heinemannlibrary.com

Printed and bound in China by South China Printing Company Limited
Photo research by Mica Brancic

09 08 07 06 05
10 9 8 7 6 5 4 3 2 1

Library of Congress Cataloging-in-Publication Data
Thomas, Isabel, 1980-
    Action art : drawing / Isabel Thomas.
        p. cm. -- (Action art)
    Includes bibliographical references and index.
    ISBN 1-4034-6918-0 (library binding-hardcover) -- ISBN 1-4034-6924-5 (pbk.)
  1. Drawing--Technique--Juvenile literature. I. Title. II. Series.
    NC655.T427 2005
    741.2--dc22

                                                      2005001578

Acknowledgments
The author and publishers are grateful to the following for permission to reproduce copyright material: Corbis pp. **5**, **6**, **17**, **19**; Getty Images pp. **14** (Stone), **18** (Taxi); Harcourt Education pp. **4**, **7**, **8**, **9**, **10**, **11**, **12**, **13**, **15**, **16**, **20**, **21**, **22**, **23**, **24** (Tudor Photography)

Cover photograph of color pencils reproduced with permission of Getty (ThinkStock)

Every effort has been made to contact copyright holders of any material reproduced in this book. Any omissions will be rectified in subsequent printings if notice is given to the publisher.

Many thanks to the teachers, library media specialists, reading instructors, and educational consultants who have helped develop the Read and Learn/Lee y aprende brand.

Some words are shown in bold, **like this**. You can find them in the picture glossary on page 23.

Contents

What Is Art?

Art is something you make when you are being **creative**.

People like to look at art.

A person who makes art is called an artist.

You can be an artist, too!

What Kinds of Art Can I Do?

There are lots of ways to create art.

You can paint and draw colorful pictures.

sculpture

You can make patterns, prints, and collage.

Sculpting is another kind of art.

7

What Is Drawing?

A drawing is a picture of something.

Drawings are made up of lines and shapes.

straight line

wavy line

This drawing has wavy lines and straight lines.

What shapes can you see?

What Can
I Draw With?

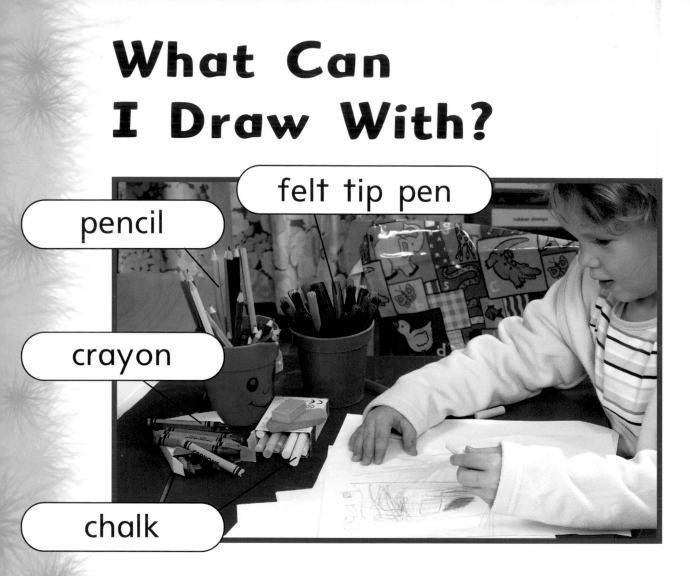

pencil

felt tip pen

crayon

chalk

You can draw with all these **tools**.

They come in many colors.

Pencils and pens make thin lines.

Crayons and chalk make thick lines.

What Can I Draw On?

You can draw on paper.

Paper comes in lots of different colors and **textures**.

You can draw on cardboard, too.

Try drawing birthday cards for your friends.

What Can I Draw?

You can draw anything that you can see.

Draw a picture of an animal or your family.

You can draw around a shape.

Try drawing around your hand.

What Else Can I Draw?

Sometimes you draw things that you **imagine**.

These children are drawing funny monsters!

Think about your favorite story.

Try to draw what you are thinking.

How Does Drawing Make Me Feel?

Drawing is fun.

It can make you feel happy.

When you **display** your drawings, you feel proud.

19

Let's Draw!

Let's draw a **portrait**!

1. Look at one of your friends. First, draw the shape of his or her head.

2. Now add the hair. Is it long or short? Is it straight or curly?

3. Draw the eyes, nose, and mouth. Look carefully at what shapes they are. Make sure you put them in the right place.

4. Now try to draw a picture of your own face!

Quiz

All of these **tools** can be used for drawing.

? ? ? ? ? ?

CRAYONS

Can you remember their names?

Look for the answers on page 24.

Picture Glossary

creative, page 4
making something using your own ideas and how you feel inside

display, page 19
put your art where people can look at it

imagine, page 16
make things up in your head

portrait, page 20
picture of somebody

texture, page 12
how something feels when you touch it

tool, page 10, 22
thing you use for coloring, such as colored pencils and crayons

Note to Parents and Teachers

Reading for information is an important part of a child's literacy development. Learning begins with a question about something. Help children think of themselves as investigators and researchers by encouraging their questions about the world around them. Each chapter in this book begins with a question. Read the question together. Look at the pictures. Talk about what you think the answer might be. Then read the text to find out if your predictions were correct. Think of other questions you could ask about the topic, and discuss where you might find the answers. Assist children in using the picture glossary and the index to practice new vocabulary and research skills.

Index

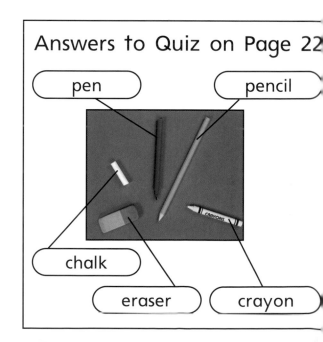

Answers to Quiz on Page 22

pen   pencil   chalk   eraser   crayon